THE A TO Z GUIDE TO THE KENYAN SAFARI

THE
KENYAN
SAFARI

ISBN 978-1-956896-00-8 (softcover)
ISBN 978-1-956896-01-5 (hardcover)
ISBN 978-1-956896-02-2 (ebook)

Printed in the United States of America.

Book Vine Press
2516 Highland Dr.
Palatine, IL 60067

THE A TO Z GUIDE TO THE KENYAN SAFARI

THE KENYAN SAFARI

your ultimate travel journal

RICHARD G MIRITI

A herd of Zebras quenching there thirst

Famous People who visited KENYA

Queen Elizabeth
Queen Elizabeth was on vacation at Treetops when she learned that her father had passed away and she was now Queen. This luxury treehouse overlooks two watering holes and has great views of Mt. Kenya The meals are eaten in the restaurant where you can watch the animals hunt, especially in the evenings or early morning when the sun is not so hot.

Bill Gates
Shompole Lodge, a luxury ecotourism lodge that overlooks the Rift Valley, is a place he has been to before.The lodge provides employment for the Maasai tribe that lives in the area. Situated near the salt lake, Lake Magadi, celebrities can catch a glimpse of the flamingoes that breed on its shores. They can also catch a glimpse of the bat-eared fox.

Prince William
He traveled to Kenya for a little vacation and decided to make Lewa his stop of choice. This luxury eco-tourist spot promotes wildelife conservation and the economic development of the region.It has been featured in Tatler Interiors, Harpers and Queen, The Times, and on BBC. Marie Claire, France, also did two of its photo shoots there.

Naomi Campbell
Naomi Campbell loved go to Lion in the Sun resort in the quiet town of Malindi, on the south coast of Kenya. Owned by her ex-boyfriend, Flavio Briattore, it is an exclusive location right on the beach.

Vanessa Williams
Vanessa Williams and Rick Fox visited Masai Mara and took in their sights at this picturesque lodge nestled in the great Rift Valley. It is famous for its lions, and the show Big Cat Diary on the BBC is filmed at this location

Editor's Note

Welcome to Kenya: The Land of Magnificent Beauty!

Jambo, Kenya is known by many as the home of the best long distance runners. Other than producing some of the best athletes in the world, this country also has beautiful tourist destinations. From the idyllic coastal region to the expansive Rift valley region, this country certainly has its fair share of magnificence! Although its known for its amazing wildlife and panoramic views, this great nation has many other aspects that make it the ultimate African safari destination. Kenya's art, bird life, cuisines and rich history are some of the aspects that guarantee tourists unrivaled safari experiences!

In this publication, we have compiled a selection of photos to showcase the ultimate Kenyan tourism experience. This photo collection captures the phenomenal Wildebeest Migration as well as the spectacular birds of Kenya. It also lists a number of destinations, recreational activities as well as the ultimate Kenyan Safari Bucket List among many other things!

This collection will take you through a journey in Kenya. Indulge and enjoy what will become of your next visit to this great African nation!

About Kenya

To start with, Kenya is the economic giant of East Africa. Our sea port supports close to seven landlocked countries in East Africa. Although Kenya's economy cannot be compared to the top ranked world economies, this nation happens to be East Africa's most preferred investment destination. Kenya harbors a number of world corporate headquarters in Africa like the United Nations Headquarters in Gigiri, Nairobi.

Kenya's infrastructural development is far much ahead of its neighbors. As the home of the first ever Mobile money transfer service, our country definitely stands out as an Information and Technology hub. This status is expected to rise as soon as the first phase of Konza City, 'African Silicon Savannah" is completed.

Intricate details such as the location of a national park within the capital city, Nairobi and numerous bird species always attract millions of visitors every year. Rare and endangered wildlife species such as the Grevy's Zebras, the African Elephant, Blue Whales, Hartebeests and Cheetahs also give visitors more reasons to visit Kenya. Additionally, this country's favorable climate also makes it ideal for safaris. Year round temperatures in most parts of the country always average at about 270C. In addition to being a perfect tourist destination, Kenya is also a perfect investment destination. We have a number of unexploited gas and oil reserves. These resources are expected to attract more foreign direct investments and in turn raise the status of our great nation. Join me and enjoy perusing this publication and discover more about Kenya, the jewel of Africa!

Karibu Kenya,

Richard Miriti

EDITOR	CONTRIBUTORS	GRAPHIC DESIGNER	ADVERTISING
Richard Miriti	Edith Wairimu	Ann Ndichu	richard@richieworld.com
richard@richieworld.com			Tel :508 -864-1609
Tel: 508 -864-1609			

A-Art

The art scene in Kenya is rich, vibrant and diverse. Kenya's art works are lucid illustrations of creativity, hard work and talent. From sculptures, to paintings, to drawings and photographs, this country simply has it all! The works of art in this country are not just a representation of individual imaginations; most of them represent the lifestyles of the different ethnic groups. What's more, Kenya has a perfect blend of natural beauty and a spectacular art scene, factors that make it an ideal Art Safari destination.

Kenya's art hubs include the Nairobi Masai Market, Kuona Trust, Wamunyu carving centre, Kitengela Glass Research and Training Trust, Osteria Art Gallery, Chungu Arts, Savio Arts, Lily Ponds Arts Centre, Nairobi Gallery, Mlango Farm Art Gallery and Lisa's Shop among many others.

The most common art works in Kenya include: soapstone carvings, wood carving, paintings, junk art, glass art, tie and dye and decorative art works.

African masks are considered amongst the finest creations in the art world and are highly sought after by art collectors

Curved Bone African Bracelet

B-Bird Watching

Kenya is a popular Bird Safari destination. According to Phoebe Snetsinger, a famous bird watching record holder, Kenya has spectacular birds which are very easy to spot. From the small Ox-peckers, white Egrets and Bustards to the powerful-sighted Eagles, the noisy Hornbills, the Ostrich and Flamingos, the largest birds on earth, Kenya definitely has amazing birdlife! This Bird Safari destination is home to an estimated 1000 bird species. Besides that, most bird watching locations are home to at least 300 bird species. Sighting about 500 bird species during brief Bird Safaris is possible in this East African nation. The most popular Bird Safari destinations in Kenya are Lake Nakuru, Lake Bogoria, Lake Baringo, Arabuko Sokoke Forest, Kakamega Forest, Sabaki River Mouth, Mida Creek, Masai Mara, Mt. Kenya, Nairobi National Park, Nairobi Ostrich Farm, Lake Jipe and Tsavo East and Tsavo West.

Yellow-billed Stork at Lake Baringo.

One subspecies of the Woodland Kingfisher breeds in Kenya

This Nubian Woodpecker was photographed at Samburu National Reserve.

C-Cuisines

The famous wildebeest migration and game drives are considered as the highlights of a Kenyan safari. During safaris, visitors always get an opportunity to enjoy some of Kenya's finest cuisines. Kenya's cuisines include ugali (which is prepared using maize flour and boiling water) which is served with sukuma wiki (kales) or beef stew. Other cuisines include wali wa nazi (coconut rice), irio (mashed potatoes and peas), githeri (corn and beans), pilau (spicy rice), chapati (wheat flour flat bread), mutura (Kenyan sausage), roasted maize, matoke, chai (tea), fish and nyama choma (roasted meat) which is Kenya's national pride.

Githeri (corn and beans)

Pilau (spicy rice)

Mutura (Kenyan sausage)

Restaurants that serve Kenyan cuisines include Kosewe's, the famous fish eatery in Nairobi, Carnivore Restaurant, Amaica Restaurant, Swahili Dishes, Malindi Dishes, Bob's Sandwich Bar and Grill, Mikaye Restaurant, Nairobi Mamba Village, Nyama Choma Ranch in Safari Park Hotel, Porini Boko Boko, Tamambo Karen Blixen Coffee Garden and Mvuli House Restaurant among many others.

The Carnivore is considered 'Africa's Greatest Eating Experience'. Every type of meat imaginable including a selection of exotic meat is roasted over charcoal and carved at your table.

D-Destinations

Kenya has for a long time been known for the phrase "Hakuna Matata" which is Swahili for "no worries". Safari, "jambo" and "karibu" are also part of the famous words that invite visitors into this magical country. In addition to hosting the phenomenal Wildebeest Migration, this classic African Safari destination is also home to some of the world's most spectacular scenes and wildlife. From the snow-capped mountains, picturesque landscapes, amazing tropical weather, magnificent birdlife, flora and fauna, heritage sites, rich history, culture and welcoming people, Kenya certainly has it all! This country's destinations are countless, welcoming and beautiful. You will never get enough of Kenya's fine destinations!

Kenya's destinations are ideal for the breathtaking hot air balloons, weddings, honeymoon, cultural tours, jungle trails, mountain climbing, plane safaris, city tours, excursions, extreme sports, game drives, fishing, water sports, sun bathing, bird watching, cultural and history exploration among many other destinations.

Samburu saruni lodge offers first-class safari experience in a totally un-spoilt environment

Siriko Camp

Treetop Lodge

Fair Mont Safari club

Destinations in Kenya that are known for their 'Royal Connection' include Treetops Hotel which is located in the Aberdares National Park, Ngwesi Eco Lodge in the Lewa Down and Rutundu Log Cabins in Mt. Kenya. Supermodel Naomi Campbell described Malindi as 'Africa' and 'an ideal relaxation destination'. Shompole Lodge, which is located in Kajiado, has hosted Bill Gates together with his family. Other famous personalities who have toured Kenya include Brad Pitt, Angelina Jolie, Bono, Reese Witherspoon, Danny DeVito and his wife Rhea Perlman among many others.

afari Camp has
ing location
ewa Wildlife
vancy, with
ding game
, and spectacular
Mt. Kenya
outh and arid
s to the north.

E-Endangered/Rare Wildlife Species

Diverse wildlife species and the numerous wildlife conserva-tion areas are some of the factors that make Kenya a perfect African Safari destination. Other than the common wildlife species, Kenya is also home to some of the world's most rare and endangered species. Out of the 5,000 Grevy's Zebras in the world, an estimated 4,300 Grevy's Zebras live in Kenya's parks and game reserves. Other endangered and rare animals include the African Elephant (about 30,000), Blue Whale (about 400), Hartebeest (about 300, the only in the world), Cheetah, Spotted Hyena and Black and White Rhinos (about 600 and 300 respectively) among many other animals.

Kenya's endangered and rare animal species can easily be sighted at the Ol Pejeta Conservancy, Sheldrick Trust's Elephant orphanage, the Rhino Sanctuary, Tsavo East National Park, Lewa Conservancy, Nairobi Animal Orphanage, Masai Mara, Nairobi National park and other game parks and reserves in the country.

F-Fishing

Kenya has numerous water masses including dams, rivers, lakes and an Ocean. These water bodies serve as perfect enya has numerous water masses including dams, rivers, lakes and an Ocean. These water bodies serve as perfect smaller water bodies, a good number of adventurous visitors prefer to try Big Game Fishing. Fly fishing, casting, trolling, bottom fishing and perking are some of the most common fishing methods in Kenya. Common fish spe-cies range from the broadbill swordfish, the trevally, the blue-stripped and black marlin, the barracuda, the kingfish, tuna, Nile perch, rainbow trout and sharks. Popular fishing areas in Kenya includes Lake Victoria, which is the source of the Nile Perch. Other fishing tour destinations include Lamu, Kiwayu, Pemba Channel, Malindi, Ras Ngomani, Watamu, Shimoni, Mt. Kenya, Aberdares National Park, Malewa, R. Thiririka, R. Chania, R. Karura, R. Gikururu, Lake Rutundu, Lake Turkana, Lake Alice and Dim-bolil.

In addition to being a perfect all-year-round fishing destination, Kenya experiences increased fishing activities during the January-March and August-December fishing seasons.

Common fishing seasons in Kenya

January-April
Most common catches at this time include blue and striped marlin and the sail fish.

May-August
August-November
Catches include Yellow-fin Tuna, blue and black marlins and sail fish.

December
Catches include sail fish, blue marlins and yellow-fin tuna.

G-Game Drives

Kenya is not just a home to the 'Big 5' wild ani-mals. This country is one of the most visited 'Great African Safari' destina tions! Game drives in this country are considered as the ultimate Kenyan adventure. The alluring beauty and majestic landscape of Kenya often invites tourists to enjoy game drives in the country's game parks and reserves. Early morning, day time and late evening game drives usher visitors into the jungle life of the elephants, black rhinos, plains zebras, buffalos, cheetahs, gazelles, impalas and hartebeests among many other wild animals.

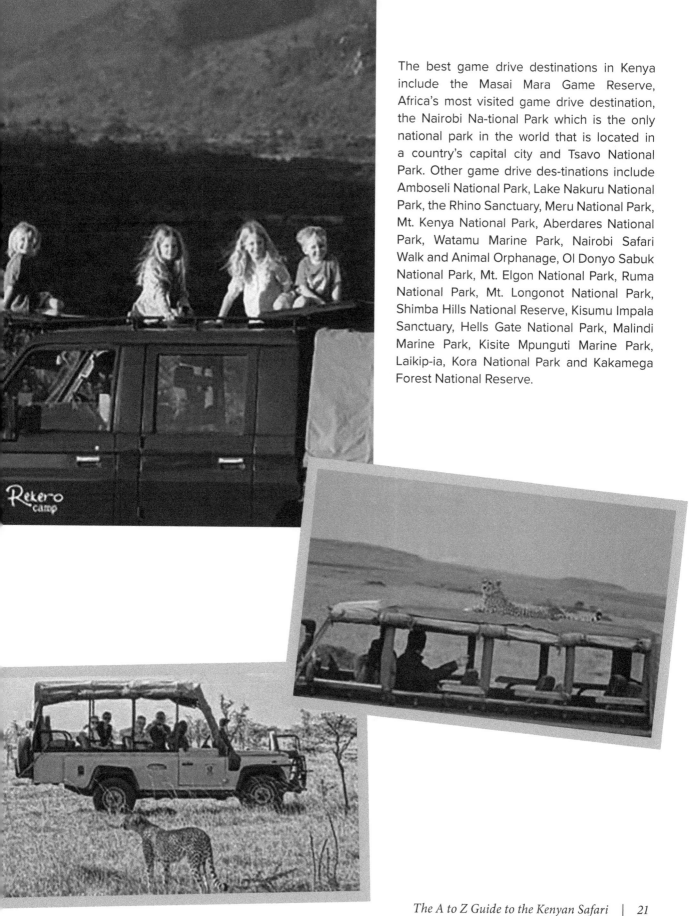

The best game drive destinations in Kenya include the Masai Mara Game Reserve, Africa's most visited game drive destination, the Nairobi Na-tional Park which is the only national park in the world that is located in a country's capital city and Tsavo National Park. Other game drive des-tinations include Amboseli National Park, Lake Nakuru National Park, the Rhino Sanctuary, Meru National Park, Mt. Kenya National Park, Aberdares National Park, Watamu Marine Park, Nairobi Safari Walk and Animal Orphanage, Ol Donyo Sabuk National Park, Mt. Elgon National Park, Ruma National Park, Mt. Longonot National Park, Shimba Hills National Reserve, Kisumu Impala Sanctuary, Hells Gate National Park, Malindi Marine Park, Kisite Mpunguti Marine Park, Laikip-ia, Kora National Park and Kakamega Forest National Reserve.

H-History

Kenya's history is rich, and interesting. This country's history is not limited to the colonial times. In addition to being the 'cradle of mankind', this country is also home to some of the most preserved cultural, architectural and historical sites. Together with the National Museums of Kenya, the Bomas of Kenya have preserved some of Kenya's best cultural aspects.

Bomas of Kenya, which is Swahili for the homesteads of Kenya, is one of the country's most visited cultural sites. This destination showcases Kenya's traditions including artifacts, dances and homes. Kenya is also home to amazing architectural historical sites that are dated back to the 15th century.

Takwa Ruins

The National Museums of Kenya

Dedan Kimathi Statue

The elephant tusks
of mombasa

Kenya's cultural and historical sites include the National Museums of Kenya which are located in different parts of the country, Gedi Ruins, Fort Jesus, Kenya National Archives, Takwa Ruins, Mombasa Old Town, Old PC Building (Nairobi Gallery), MacMillan Library, Uhuru Gardens, Kipande House, Vasco Da Gama Pillar, the German Post Office Museum, the Lamu Archipalego, Jomo Kenyatta Monument, Dedan Kimathi Statue, the elephant tusks of Mombasa, Mau Mau freedom war and landmarks and the Bomb Blast Memorial Park in Nairobi.

The lamu
archipalego

I-Indian Ocean

Located about 500km from Nairobi-Kenya's capital city, the Indian Ocean and its environs always stand out as perfect tourist destinations. This region's warmth, appeal and mighty grandeur always spell out "karibu" to all people while inviting everyone to relax and indulge. In addition to hav-ing a 480km-long coastline, marine parks, resorts, parks, birds, museums, national heritage and historical sites, this region also serves as the seaport to a number of East African countries. The Lamu Port and South Sudan Ethiopia Transport (LAPSSET) Corridor, which is currently under construction, is expected to open this exotic paradise up to more cruise and cargo ships.

Popular destinations in Kenya's Coastal region include Watamu, Pemba Channel, Ras Ngomani, Kiwayu, Malindi, Lamu and Shimoni which are the region's best fishing destinations, Lamu town, the historical and Swahili Cultural Hub, Diani Beach, the classic Coastal tropical paradise, Mida Creek, the bird watcher's paradise, Arabuko Sokoke Forest, Sabaki River Mouth, Gedi Ruins, Vasco Da Gama Pillar, Mombasa Tusks, Tiwi Beach, Jumba la Mtwana, Kipepeo Project and Fort Jesus among many others.

J-Jungle Adventures

The jungle in Kenya is majestic, enviable and picture perfect to say the least! From the open savannah land to grasslands and mountainous areas, this country indeed has perfect locations for jungle adventures. Jungle adventures in Kenya range from butterfly watching, walking safaris, bird watching, cave excursions and camping. Life in the jungle is often epitomized by breathtaking sunsets, bush dining, jungle trails and overnight camping. These and more factors confirm that Kenya is a perfect embodiment of what jungle safaris should be like.

Hells Gate

Best cave excursion destinations include Kitum caves. These caves are located in the slopes of Mt Elgon. Elephants mostly go into these caves at night to scrape cave walls that are a great source of salt. Other caves include the Shimoni Slave Caves, which are situated next to Shimoni Pier, the historic Mau Mau caves, Mt Suswa caves, Kisula Complex Caves in Chyulu Hills (the world's deepest lava tube caves in the world), Paradise Lost, Kit Mikayi rock, the rock of Nzambani, Oloolua Nature Trail, Karura Forest caves and Kenyatta caves among many others.

Best camping destinations are Mt. Kenya National Park, Mwea National Park, Kisumu Impala Sanctuary, Lake Nakuru National Park, Sibiloi National Park, Hell's Gate National Park, Ruma National Park, Tsavo East and West National Parks, Mt. Elgon National Park, Masai Mara National Reserve, Nairobi National Park, Amboseli National Park and Aberdare National Park amongst others. Other camping sites include Naivasha Kongoni Lodge, Moonlight Village, Thompson's Falls Lodge Camp site, Acacia Camp, Swara Plains, Camp Carnelley's, Mara Bush House, Kembu Farm, Paradise Lost, Sweetwater's Tented Camp, Rapids Camp Sagana, Fisherman's Camp Naivasha, Ndololo Tented camp and Kianjata Springs camp.

K-Kenya National Heritage Sites

Kenya is no ordinary tourist destination country. This tourist destination is also the "Cradle of Mankind"! In addition to being home to about 1000 human fossils, it is also home to oldest fossils. The oldest fossils were recovered from the Turgen Hills in Baringo and they are about 7 million years old. Apart from that, Kenya also has some of the world's most complete skeletons which include the Turkana boy. Other than the fascinating human evolution evidence this nation also has amazing heritage sites. These sites include historical sites and monuments. The most popular archeological sites in Kenya include Koobi Fora Museum, Loiyangalani, Olorgesailie, Kitum Caves, Makingeny Caves, Fort Jesus, Kitale, Mfangano Island, Malaba, Nairobi National Museum and other museums, Kisumu, Lake Turkana, El Molo Bay, Bomas of Kenya, Kariandusi, Gedi Ruins, Manda Island, Lamu and the Hyrax Hill which is situated near Nakuru. The monuments of Kenya include Vasco Da Gama Pillar in Malindi, Sir Badden Powell Grave in Nyeri, Dedan Kimathi monument in the Capital City Nairobi, Tom Mboya monument, Uhuru Garden's Memorial monument, Dinosaur Statue which is located in the Nairobi National Museum, Jomo Kenyatta statue, Kenyatta House in Maralal, Kenya Independence monument and the Jomo Kenyatta Mausoleum which is located within the parliament buildings compound.

L-Landscape

Kenya is known as the 'land of great contrasts'. This country's landscape is so diverse that Kenya is often referred to as "all of Africa in one country". Kenya's diverse landscape ranges from snow-capped mountains to plains, deserts, plateaus, coastal dry forests, rain forests and the Great Rift Valley, which has divided the country into two halves. Kenya's water bodies on the other hand, occupy two thirds of the country's total area (582,646 km2). In addition to that, Kenya is also home to every other landform type including Equatorial, Aeolian, Savannah, Volcanic, Glacial, and Tectonic territories.

Kenya's most interesting landscapes include the Great Rift Valley. The Great Rift Valley is particularly interesting because of its measurements. The 65-kmwide and 609-m-deep formation is the source of some of Kenya's lakes and rivers. Mt. Kenya, the country's dormant volcanic mountain, the Indian Ocean, Lakes Baringo and Bogoria, which are home to the largest population of larger and smaller Flamingos and the hilly Eastern region. Essentially, Kenya's landscape is broadly categorized as the Coastal belt and plains, Foreland plateau, the Northern plain lands, the highlands, the Coastal Hinterlands and the Nyanza low plateau. All of these landscapes have breathtaking scenes that enhance the experiences of most visitors.

M-Mountain Climbing

Standing at 5,199m, Kenya's highest dormant volcano mountain, Mt. Kenya is one of the most popular mountain climbing destinations. This destination has a perfect blend of scenic landscapes, mountain vegetation, amazing birdlife, wildlife and perfect trekking tracks. In addition to being Kenya's "rooftop", Mt. Kenya is also home to breathtaking ridges, cliffs and peaks. Point Lenana, one of the peaks on this mountain, offers mountain climbers a spectacular view of Mt. Kilimanjaro, Mt. Elgon and Kenya's coastal region at sunrise. The highlights of mountain climbing, jungle treks or nature trails in Kenya include bird watching, camping and the thrill associated with jungle adventures.

The best time to climb Mt. Kenya to the Batian peak is between August and September. This peak is best accessed through the North Face Standard Route. Climbing to Nelion peak is easier between December and January via the Mackinder's Route. Other ideal mountain climbing destinations in Kenya include Mt. Longonot, Ngong Hills, Mt. Olorgesailie, Aberdares ranges, Mt. Elgon, Karura Caves and Waterfalls, Hell's Gate, Suswa Crater and caves, Lukenya Hills, Mt. Kulal, Ol Donyo Sabuk, Lewis Glaciers and Kereita cave and waterfalls.

N-Nightlife

The end of a day in Kenya is mostly characterized by an amazing sunset in most parts of the country. As the sun goes down, darkness ushers in a host of vibrant activities. The energy and vigor in most towns is often heightened at this time thanks to the numerous entertainment spots. In addition to being vibrant, this country's nightlife is well known for it's 'anything goes attitude". While some people prefer to spend their evenings in bars and nightclubs, a good number of people spend their time in movie theatres, sports stadiums, restaurants, casinos, shopping complexes, concerts or house parties. Kenya's nightlife offers each individual a unique way of unwinding after a long day. What's more, individuals always have an opportunity to create their ideal 'perfect night'!

A night out in one of Kenya's entertainment spots makes for a truly unforgettable moment for most visitors. Located in every other part of the country, these entertainment spots always ensure that revelers have a great time. Kenya's shopping malls always open their doors to movie lovers and shoppers while sports stadiums keep the competitive spirit high even after dark. Basically, your night in Kenya is your responsibility. Make it a night to remember!

O-Ornaments

Ornaments in Kenya are not just beauty accessories! In some cultures, ornaments are symbols of a status, age group or wealth. Kenyan ornaments are mostly associated with the nomadic communities of Kenya like the Maasai, Turkana, Pokot, Rendile and Nandi among many others. Other communities also make and wear traditional ornaments. While cultural practices tell the stories of Kenyan people, their ornaments always express their values explicitly.

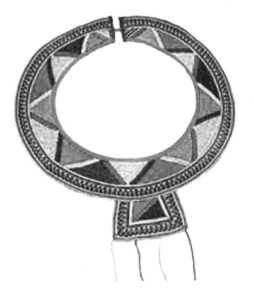

One authentic Handmade Maasai Wedding Necklace. This collar necklace are traditionally worn by Maasai women during weddings and special tribal occasions. Colorful Maasai seed beads are stitched on hard untreated hide using wire and thread.

This tribal bracelet is hand bea by the Maasai women of Ke This exquisite piece of Ma culture is a work of art. The brac is made of seed beads care woven together with wire thre and fastened with a wire hoo

Interacting with different communities is the easiest way of learning about the different types of ornaments. Most local communities make necklaces, bangles, head pieces, beads and rings.

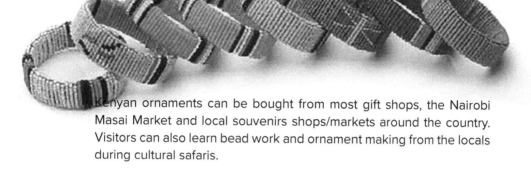

Kenyan ornaments can be bought from most gift shops, the Nairobi Masai Market and local souvenirs shops/markets around the country. Visitors can also learn bead work and ornament making from the locals during cultural safaris.

Maasai Sandals
They are made from Camel Leather then its decorated with bead work. There variety of designs created with wonderful beads

Maasai beaded Belt

Earings and Bracelets
Hand-beaded earrings Each earring having a slightly varied beaded design which can be custome made as per clients desire. Bracelets can be made to be of different heights

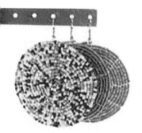

P-People and Culture

Kenya is home to 42 ethnic groups and millions of immigrants. Each of the 42 ethnic groups has unique culture and cultural activities. The diversity in cultures makes Kenya an ideal cultural safari destination. A cultural safari gives a visitor an opportunity to engage directly with local residents. Cultural safaris are intended to give visitors a chance to learn and understand the most intricate aspects of a specific culture through active participation. Cultural safaris are mostly characterized by visits to villages, participation in a village's day-today activities, eating, singing and dancing among many other

day-to-day activities. Cultural safaris are the most effective way of teaching about the people of Kenya and their cultures. These safaris are mostly organized by travel firms upon request. The highlights of a cultural safari include meeting new people and learning a new culture.

Q-Quiet Time Zones

Away from the boisterous jungle, busy towns and vibrant entertainment spots, lies some of Kenya's most tranquil spots. These spots offer every individual an opportunity to unwind in the best way possible. The multiple quiet zones in Kenya are located in different parts of the country and are always open to visitors. What's more, these zones serve as perfect locations for different types of functions including weddings, private family functions, business meetings, picnics, parties, dining and general relaxation. Picnic sites like Paradise Lost and Arboretum gardens are some of the ideal quiet zones in Kenya. Some resorts and camping sites also offer the same comfort to individuals. Massage parlors and spa treatment centres are also perfect relaxation areas. Some of Kenya's resorts, hotels and camping sites also serve as perfect locations for intimate, formal and family functions.

Alfajiri is one of the most stylish and exclusive villas in the world and set in a beautiful position overlooking a peaceful stretch of the white sands of the Diani Beach on Mombasa's south coast.

Delta Dunes Lodge sits atop tall windswept dunes at the old mouth of Kenya's mighty Tana River. This is an utterly unique lodge, set on a long stretch of beautiful unspoilt Kenya coastline.

R-Rafting and other Water Sports

Kenya's coastline is fine and magical. Thousands of visitors tour the coastal region to relax by the ocean, but that's not all! A large group of other visitors also get an opportunity to participate in thrilling water sports. Some of the most popular water sports in Kenya include scuba diving, snorkeling, deep sea diving and surfing. This country's coastline is perfect for water sports because it is well secured by coral reefs. Protected areas serve as ideal water sport spots. Malindi and Mombasa have spots that are ideal for diving adventures. Lamu Island on the other hand is perfect for snorkeling and playing with dolphins. Other exciting water sports in Kenya's coastal region include boat riding, dhow races and fishing competitions. The Rapids Camp in Sagana is also perfect for rafting, bungee jumping, plunging, kayaking and gliding among many other recreational water sports. Most lakes and rivers in Kenya also provide tourists with recreational water sports services.

kisite-mpunguti-marine-park

S-Shopping

The shopping scene in Kenya has been changing drastically in the past few years. In addition to experiencing an increase in markets and supermarkets, this country has also registered a dramatic increase in online shops and malls. Kenya's shops are easy to locate and access. Located in strategic parts of major towns and residential areas, malls and open-air markets provide residents and visitors with one-stop-shopping solutions for food, clothing, jewelry, appliances, services and souvenirs among many other items.

Kenya's most popular open-air markets include Muthuruwa, Gikomba, Toi, Maasai, Marikiti and Ngara markets. Major shopping malls include Nakumatt Nyali, City Mall Nyali and Nakumatt Likoni in Mombasa, Westgate, Sarit Centre, the Village Market, the Junction, Thika Road, Galleria, T-Mall and Nakumatt Lifestyle in Nairobi. Other malls are located in Nanyuki, Kisumu, Eldoret, Embu and Nakuru towns.

T-The Kenyan Safari Ultimate Bucket List

1 Hot air balloon ride at the Mara during the wildebeest migration

3 Visit to Lamu; Kenya's oldest historic town

2 Train ride from the country's capital to your preferred destination

4 Bird watching at Mida Creek, Sabaki River Mouth, Kakamega Forest or the Nairobi National Park.

5 Camping in the jungle.

6 Visit to a park make sure that you spot the Big 5 including the rare White Rhino.

7 A road trip to nowhere in particular, as long as you trace your way back to your hotel room!

8 A night out in one of the capital city's night clubs. Party hard!

9 Go for shopping. You must get evidence to take back home to your friends!

10 Conquer one of your greatest fears: feeding wild animals, deep sea diving, bungee jumping etc.

11 Sightseeing at the Fourteen Falls and Chania Falls in Thika, Karura Falls, Thompson Falls and Gura Falls in the Aberdares National Park, Adamson's falls in the Koru National Park, Lugard Forest in Tsavo East National Park and Limuru Falls.

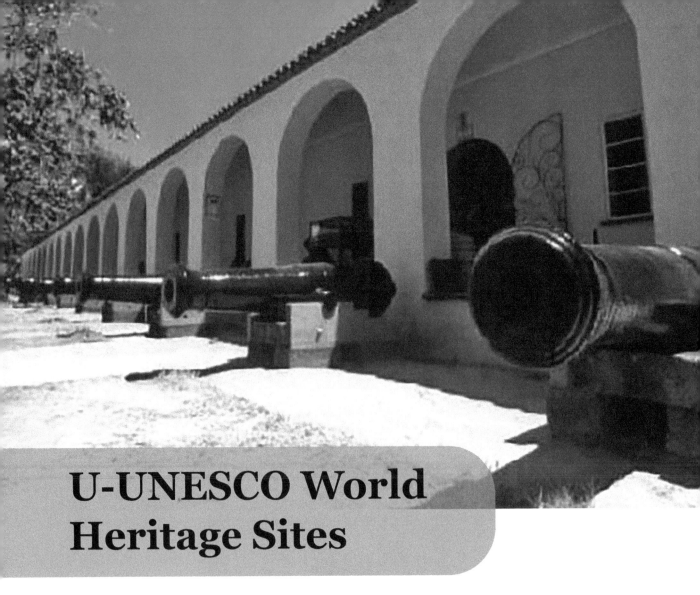

U-UNESCO World Heritage Sites

Kenya is home to a host of cultural and natural sites that have been recognized and listed as UNESCO World Heritage sites. These sites are some of Kenya's most visited tourist destinations. The World Heritage sites in Kenya include Lake Baringo, Lake Elementaita and Lake Nakuru, the birds and Flamingo paradises, Mt. Kenya, Mt. Kenya National Park, Sibiloi National Park and Lake Turkana National Park, Lamu, Central Island, the Sacred Mijikenda Kaya Forests and Fort Jesus.

Mt. Kenya

Flamingo paradises

Fort Jesus.

Lamu

W-Wildebeest Migration

The dramatic yet breathtaking wildebeest migration is an amazing spectacle. In addition to being listed as one of the "Seven new wonders of the world", this act of nature has set Kenya apart as a unique African safari destination! During the great wildebeest migration, about 1.3 million wildebeests, zebras and gazelles cross the Mara River and head to Serengeti National Park in search of water and greener pastures. Watching the wildebeest migration on a hot air balloon always makes the experience more exciting. The highlight of the migration is watching zebras, wildebeests and gazelles as they attempt to cross the crocodile-infested Mara river as thousands of other predators wait to prey on the weaker animals.

Best time to watch the Great wildebeest migration in Masai Mara

The migration pattern is always dependent on the Mara ecosystem seasons. Despite the occasional season changes in the Mara, a few wildebeests start arriving in Masai Mara in July. The main migration of the wildebeests into Kenya however, takes place between August and September and goes on between October and November. Migration of wildebeests to Serengeti takes place between December and January.

X-Xtreme Sports

Extreme recreational sports are a source of adventure and thrill. These sports push individuals to their limits and also create a great sense of fulfillment in those who emerge as conquerors. All extreme sports participants in Kenya are usually supervised by trained staff to prevent avoidable accidents. As a safety measure, extreme sports are always held in the right locations and during the ideal weather.

Some of the most popular extreme recreational sports in Kenya include paragliding in Turkana. Other extreme recreational sports include deep sea diving in the country's coastal region, bungee jumping at the Rapids Camp in Sagana, rock climbing at Kit Mikayi, Nzambani rock and Kenya's hilly regions, surfing and rafting in most of Kenya's inland water bodies.

Transport

Getting into and around Kenya is easy thanks to the advanced transport system. This country has a wide network of modern airports, railway line and roads. This country's main airports include the Jomo Kenyatta International Airport in Nairobi, Moi International Airport in Mombasa and Kisumu Airport in Kisumu. Rift Valley Railways provides train services from Nairobi, Kenya's capital to major towns. The road network in Kenya comprises of a by-pass network, which was constructed to help ease traffic and facilitate easy accessibility of Nairobi and its environs. Kenya's transport system is also served by international, national, primary and secondary roads as well as sea and inland transport.

Transport options within Kenya include:

Taxis - Africabs, 24/7 cabs, Royal Cabs, Princess Cab and Car Hire Ltd, Jim Cab Services Charter Aircrafts - Excel Aviation, Z-Boskovic Air Charters and Blue Bird Aviation Commercial airlines - Kenya Airways, AirKenya, Safarilink, Air France, British Airways Buses - Eldoret Express, Modern Coast, Dreamline, Kenya Bus Services, Easy Coach Tour vans - usually provided by travel agencies Rental cars - Rent-a-Car, Budget, Hertz, Avis among many others Train - Rift Valley Railways Boats, cruise ships, ferries, dhows and canoes among many others

Sleep in Kenya's Finest Hotels

Tafaria Castle and Country Lodge - Located on a hill close to the Aberdare Ranges, this lodge offers residents a perfect view of Mt. Kenya and the expansive Laikipia Plains. In addition to being the perfect stop over for visitors who love game watching, bird watching, golfing and fishing, this lodge is particularly popular because of its medieval architectural design. This 29-room lodge is a perfect stop over for tourists on their way to Masai Mara, Mt. Kenya, Samburu and the Western part of Kenya among many other tourist destinations. Guests who book the Lord's Room are always crowned the Lord of the Tafaria Castle for a day. Other rooms include the Knights' quarters, the Damsels' Quarters, the Lost Knights' Quarters, the Old-House and the Vikings' Quarters.

Enashipai Resort and Spa – Enashipai Resort and Spa is situated in Naivasha, the bird watcher's paradise in Kenya. The beauty in this resort is a perfect blend of nature, history and culture. Enashipai, which is the Maasai word for 'a place of happiness', offers a tranquil, luxurious and comfortable home away from home to all its residents. This resort has spacious cottages and executive rooms which are surrounded by breathtaking views of the nearby rolling hills and beautiful gardens. Tourist attractions that are close to this resort include Mt. Longonot and Hells Gate, which are perfect for hiking adventures, Lake Naivasha National Park and Lake Naivasha, the home of Kenya's highest population of flamingos.

Sankara Luxury Hotel - Ranked 8th in the Trip Advisor's, Travelers Choice 2013 -Top 25 Hotels in Kenya, Sankara certainly stands out as an extraordinaire hotel. Located in Westlands, a few minutes' drive from the country's capital city Nairobi, this luxury hotel serves as a perfect haven for both leisure and business travelers. This 5-star hotel boasts of contemporary interior designs and modern room facilities. With a total of 156 luxury rooms and suites, Sankara always invites individuals to indulge in world-class luxury. Some of the popular destinations near this hotel include the Nairobi National Museum, the Nairobi National Park, Giraffe Centre, Mamba Village, David Sheldrick's Elephant Orphanage and Uhuru Park among many others.

Sarova Mara Game Camp - Located within the Masai Mara ecosystem, this game camp is considered as one of the best places to stay within Africa's most famous jungle, Masai Mara Game Reserve. This camp offers game watchers a rare opportunity to witness the phenomenal Wildebeest Migration, one of the seven new wonders of the world. A stay in this camp also gives individuals a chance to come close to Kenya's wildlife in their habitats. Sarova Mara Game Camp is synonymous with bush adventure. In addition to enjoying game drives in the Masai Mara, residents in this tented camp always get an opportunity to enjoy bush meals, fishing, traditional dances and music and bird watching among many other recreational activities. Sarova Mara Game Camp has 20 club tents, 51 standard tents and 2 family tents. Baby sitting services are also available.

Turtle Bay Club Watamu - The Turtle Bay Club lies on a 10-acre piece of land next to the Indian Ocean. This hotel also boasts of a 200-metres-long beach which hosts recreational activities such as wind surfing, basking and scuba diving among many other activities. The 145 en-suite rooms in this hotel are served by three bars, three restaurants and two swimming pools. In the Trip Advisor's 2013 Top 25 Hotels in Kenya list, this beach hotel is captioned as one of the places every person should visit! Located next to one of the world's most popular marine parks, Watamu Marine Park, the Turtle Bay Club gives individuals easy access to the beach and the marine park. Visitors also get an opportunity to witness the nesting of three endangered turtle species.

Mnarani Beach Club - This intimate beach resort is located about 60 kms North of Mombasa, Kenya's coastal town. This 27-rooms resort lies on 40 acres of lush tropical gardens next to the Indian Ocean. Mnarani Beach Club is strategically located on a cliff. Apart from enjoying garden views, residents always enjoy perfect ocean and cliff views. The Indian Ocean and Kilifi Creek, serve as a perfect spot for water sports such as sailing, water boarding, water skiing, scuba diving and snorkeling among many other activities. Accommodation in this beach resort is provided in wellbuilt cottages that range from small, standard to deluxe cottages. Mnarani Beach is perfect for family vacations as well as romantic getaways.

Amboseli Serena Safari Lodge – Located within the Amboseli ecosystem, the Amboseli Serena Safari lodge stands out as one of the best safari lodges in Kenya. Other than offering world-class services, this lodge gives visitors an opportunity to enjoy great ambience, food, landscape and wildlife. Mt. Kilimanjaro, Africa's highest mountain, casts its majestic shadows over the lodge as natural springs bring to life the beauty of life in the surrounding ecosystem. The Amboseli National Park which is home to the largest elephant population in Africa also makes a stay in this lodge more memorable. Wild animals such as baboons, buffalos, giraffes, cheetahs, lions, wildebeests and gazelles also add thrill to an individual's stay.

Sweetwaters Tented Camp, Nanyuki – The rolling plains of Kenya's highest mountain, Mt. Kenya, are home to one of Kenya's largest private wildlife conservancies, Ol Pejeta Conservancy. Sweetwaters Tented Camp is situated in the heart of this conservancy. The Sweetwaters camp has 39 luxury tents which provide home to visitors in the jungle. All tents have a patio which gives a view of the 'watering hole'. The high wildlife ratio in the conservancy makes the 'watering hole' the perfect spot for wildlife viewing throughout the day. The traditional set up of the camp, fine cuisine, birds, cultural music and dances are some of the highlights visitors

enjoy during their stay in the camp. Other than hosting safari tourists, this camp also serves as a perfect location for weddings and honeymoons.

Sasaab Camp – Located within the Westgate Community Conservancy, the Sasaab Camp stands out as a perfect getaway location. This beautiful camp lies on half a mile of land mass next to the Samburu National Reserve. This Camp has nine spacious rooms which offer a view of the third largest river, Ewaso Nyiro. The open patios in each camp also give individuals the rare view of wildlife in their natural habitat. Other than the scenic landscape around the camp, the fascinating camel rides, trips to the famous Samburu market and game drives, this camp ushers visitors into the home of the endangered Grevy's Zebra species.

Campi ya Kanzi – The pristine bush at the foot of the famous Chyulu Hills in the Southern Part of Kenya is home to a large number of wild animals. With over 60 wild mammal species, 1000 plant species and more than 400 bird species, this location stands out as a perfect safari location. Accommodation at the gold-rated ecotourism Campi ya Kanzi gives individuals a chance to experience life in the jungle. Located between the famous Amboseli and Tsavo National parks, this camp certainly gives tourists an authentic African safari experience. The perfect view of Mt. Kilimanjaro, interaction with the Maasai community, jungle dining and game drives definitely make for a great vacation for everyone living in this lovely camp.

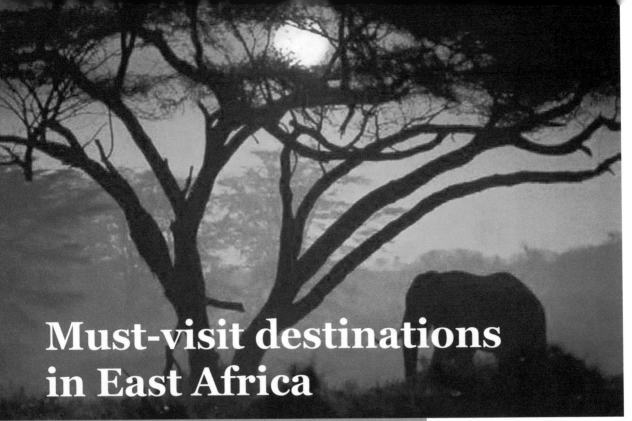

Must-visit destinations in East Africa

Tanzania's Finest Destinations

Serengeti National Park
Fact File
Location: Northern Tanzania
Size: 14,750km2
Known for: The largest wildlife population and the famous Wildebeest migration Common wild animals include: Lions, black rhinos, African leopards, African elephants and wildebeests. This park is one of the UNESCO World Heritage Sites in Tanzania.

Udzungwa Mountains National Park
Fact File
Location: South East of Dodoma in Tanzania
Size: 1,990km2
Height: 2,579m
Known for: High biodiversity and a large population of mammals such as the Tana River Mangabey, the Udzungwa Red Colobus and the Grey-faced Sengi among many other wildlife species.
The Udzungwa Mountains National Park is referred to as the Galapagos Islands of Africa. This park is part of the larger Eastern Arc Mountains which stretch over 10,000km2. The Udzungwa Mountains National Park is listed as one of the 34 World Biodiversity Hotspots as well as one of the eco-regions of critical global importance.

Ngorongoro Crater
Fact File
Location: Crater Highland in Tanzania
Size: 300km2 (20kms wide and 600m deep)
Known for: Panoramic views and a variety of wildlife species The Ngorongoro Crater is the largest inactive volcanic caldera in the world. This crater has three dominant regions, the crater highland, the grassland and the crater floor. These regions are home to a number of wild animals including the famous Big 5.

Mt. Kilimanjaro
Fact File
Location: Mt. Kilimanjaro National Park in Tanzania
Height: 5,895m
Known for: Seven amazing trekking routes, panoramic views of the surrounding and scenic camping sites
Mt. Kilimanjaro is the highest mountain in Africa and the tallest free standing mountain in the world. This mountain has three cones: Shira 3,962m, Kibo 5,895m and Mawenzi 5,149m. The highest point on this mountain is located within the Kibo crater.

Uganda's Finest Destinations

Semliki National Park and Wildlife Reserve

Fact File

Location: Bundibugyo District along the Uganda-DRC (Democratic Republic of Congo) border.

Size: 221km2

Known for: Rich birdlife (over 400 bird species). More than 60 per cent of Uganda's true forest bird species are found in this park.

Semliki National Park and Wildlife Reserve is one of the most popular bird watching destinations in Uganda. This park is part of the Albertine Rift Valley protected areas. Neighboring Lake Albert and Rwenzori mountains are also part of the Albertine Rift Valley.

Bwindi National Park

Fact File

Location: South West part of Uganda along the Uganda-DRC (Democratic Republic of Congo) border.

Size: 331km2

Known for: Its title, 'the home of the mountain gorillas'. The population of mountain gorillas at the Bwindi National Park stands at 340. This number accounts for nearly half of the total global mountain gorilla population.

Bwindi is one of the UNESCO World Heritage Sites in Uganda. This park is the natural habitat to more than 10 gorilla species. Bwindi National Park is also home to more than 200 butterfly species and close to 350 forest bird species. This park serves as a perfect gorilla tracking location.

Rwenzori Mountains

Fact File

Location: Across Kabarole, Kasese and Bundibugyo Districts in Uganda.

Size: 1000km2 (120km along the Uganda-DRC border)

Height: Highest point (5, 109m)

Known for: The title, 'the mountains of the moon'. This mountain range has a total of six mountains. The highest peak, which is situated on Mt Stanley's stands at 5, 109m. In addition to being Africa's third highest peak, this mountain range also has a number of panoramic waterfalls, glaciers and lakes.

The Rwenzori mountain range is listed as a UNESCO World Heritage Site. It is a popular mountain climbing destination. It takes approximately 10 days to conquer the rough yet fascinating terrain to the highest peak on the range.

Queen Elizabeth National Park

Fact File

Location: Across Kamwenge, Kasese, Rukungiri and Bushenyi Districts (376km from Kampala, Uganda's capital city).

Size: 1,978km2

Known for: Game drive experiences that are out of the ordinary. Queen Elizabeth National Park is known by many as the 'true jungle'. Located within the park, the Kasenyi track gives tourists an opportunity to see wild animals such as lions, leopards, elephants and warthogs among many others.

With over 600 bird species, Queen Elizabeth National Park certainly stands out as a perfect bird watching destination. The Kyambura Gorge, which is situated within the park, offers visitors extraordinary bird watching experiences. This location is also perfect for chimpanzee tracking. The Kazinga Channel is the perfect for hippopotamus watching. Most of the world's hippo population is found in this channel.

Rwanda's Finest Destinations

Akagera National Park

Fact File

Location: In Nyagatare on the North-Eastern part of Rwanda along the Rwanda-Tanzania border.

Size: 1,200km2

Known for: Scenic views of the vast savannah jungle, the mountain region as well as the swampy area. Akagera National Park is also known for its beautiful landscape and natural park vegetation.

The Akagera National Park is home to more than 500 migrant and resident bird species. It is also home to topis, elephants, zebras, hippos, lions, primates, buffalos and giraffes among many other wild animals. This park is both a bird watcher's and game drive paradise.

Nyungwe Rainforest

Fact File

Location: South-Western side of Rwanda along the Rwanda-Burundi border

Size: 1000km2

Known for: A spectacular 200m canopy walk, more than 13 primate species and close to 300 bird species.

Nyungwe Rainforest is also Rwanda's main water catchment area and the source of rivers Nile and Congo, Africa's greatest rivers. Nyungwe National Park, which is part of the larger Nyungwe Rainforest, is also home to more than 80 mammal species, numerous butterfly species, forest vegetation and insects.

Nyungwe Rainforest is a popular hiking destination. This destination is also ideal for nature walks and camping. Apart from being Africa's largest mountain rainforest, this forest has rich biodiversity, a factor that makes it a unique safari destination in Rwanda.

Volcanoes National Park

Fact File

Location: North-Western part of Rwanda along the Rwanda-DRCUganda border.

Size: 160km2

Altitude: 2,400km to 4,507km

Known for: Its mountain gorilla population and a wide variety of vegetation. The Volcanoes National Park is also home to five of Virunga Mountain's eight volcanoes. This park has an estimated 175 bird species and is considered as one of the best gorilla tracking and hiking destinations in Rwanda.

More than 70 mammal species including the endangered golden monkeys live in the Volcanoes National Park. In addition to having the largest density of the East African Rosewood plant, this park is also listed as one of the two locations where tracking habituated gorillas can be done in the world.

Kigali Genocide Memorial Centre
Fact File
Location: Kigali, Rwanda
Known for: Its role in the articulate documentation of the infamous and devastating 1994 Rwanda Genocide. The Kigali Genocide Memorial Centre is known for the role it plays in advocating for peace.

The Kigali Genocide Memorial Centre stands on the site where more than 200,000 Tutsis were buried during the 100-day violence which resulted in the deaths of more than one million people. This centre is definitely a must-visit site for anyone who visits Rwanda as it emphasizes the importance of unity among people from different backgrounds.

King of the Jungle

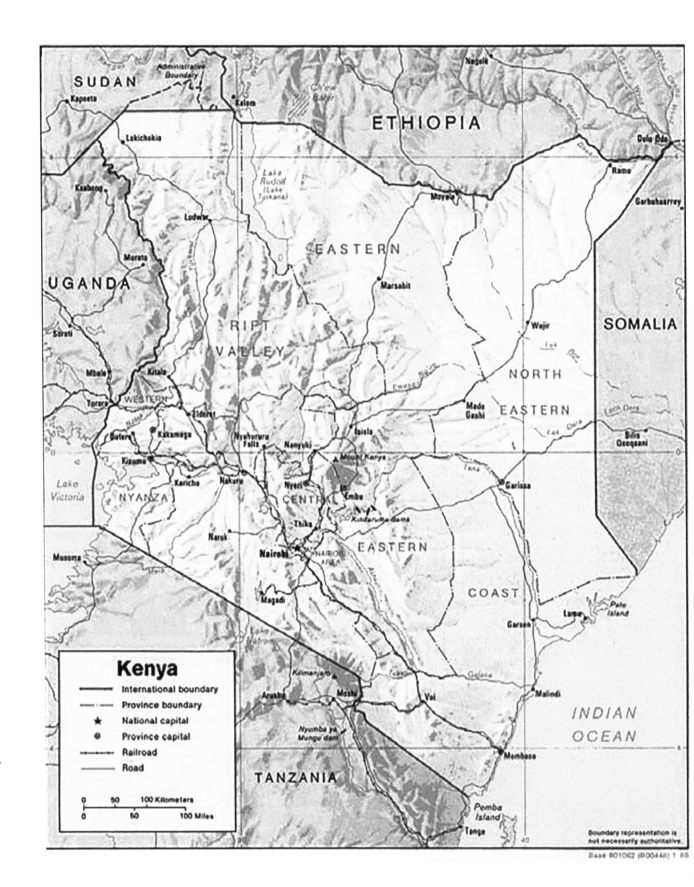

Administrative Map of Kenya

Kilometers

Major Port
Capital City
Major towns

PROVINCES
CENTRAL
COAST
EASTERN
NAIROBI
NORTH EASTERN
NYANZA
RIFT VALLEY
WESTERN

Map by WFP/VAM, Kenya

The boundaries and names shown and the designations used on this map
do not imply official endorsement or acceptance by the United Nations.

CPSIA information can be obtained
at www.ICGtesting.com
Printed in the USA
LVHW070119150422
716160LV00002B/7